THE BOOK OF STEVE

written by
Steve Robertson

*Dedicated to every man
learning that strength and love
are not opposites, but partners –
and living with a disability
doesn't have to destroy your manhood.*

THE BOOK OF STEVE

Written By
Steve Robertson

Cover Image By
Tisha Ann

Fullcover Design By
Sun Child Wind Spirit

Proofread By
Latisha Jefferson-Robertson

Edited By
Mylia Tiye Mal Jaza

THE BOOK OF STEVE
Copyright © 2026, Steve Robertson
All Rights Reserved.

Softback ISBN 10: 7231731902
Softback ISBN 13: 9784792174903

This art is a book of non-fiction. No part of this work may be reproduced or transmitted in any form or by any means (graphic, electronic, magnetic, photographic, or mechanical - including photocopying, recording, taping, or by any information storage/retrieval system) without the written permission of the author/publisher. Post demise of author/ publisher, then valid permission for reproduction and transmittal must be obtained from multiple immediate/major survivors of the author's family. Although careful preparation of this work permeated every phase, it is understood that perfection is humanly impossible. Further, the content of this book does not serve as professional counseling. Thus, neither the self-publishing associate, author/publisher nor imprinter accepts liability for errors, omissions, nor damages resulting from the use of any information presented herein.

Author
Steve Robertson
latishajefferson2@gmail.com
Facebook.com/profile.php?id=100076496012717

Self-Publishing Associate
Dr. Mary M. Jefferson
BePublished.Org - Chicago, IL
(972) 880-8316
www.bepublished.org

First Edition.
Printed In the USA
Recycled Paper Encouraged.

Table of Contents

Chapter 1 — November 16, 1978: Where My Story Began 9
Early life, family, and the foundations that shaped who I am

Chapter 2 — Lessons Learned the Hard Way 16
Challenges, mistakes, and experiences that tested my strength

Chapter 3 — The Importance of Life 24
Moments that changed my perspective and taught me the value of living with purpose

Chapter 4 — Growth, Faith, and Self-Discovery 31
How reflection, belief, and personal growth reshaped my path

Chapter 5 — Becoming Steven Robertson 38
Finding identity, resilience, and meaning through lived experience

Chapter 6 — Looking Forward: The Life I Choose 43
Hope, wisdom gained, and the message I want to leave behind

Chapter 7 — Choosing Health, Choosing Love 48
Hope, wisdom gained, and the message I want to leave behind

50 Ways To Be A BEST Man 56
Tips to live a life that shows masculinity and affection to those you love

The Art & Artists 63

CHAPTER 1
November 16, 1978: Where My Story Began

I was born on November 16, 1978, a date that would come to mean more to me as I got older than it ever did in the beginning. Like most people, I didn't arrive in this world with an understanding of what life would ask of me, what it would take from me, or what it would demand that I become. I came into life simply breathing, crying, and existing — unaware that I would spend decades learning what it truly means to live.

When I look back now, I don't remember the moment of my birth, but I remember the feeling of growing up — how early life felt like a mixture of safety and confusion, comfort and uncertainty. Childhood has a way of disguising reality. You live inside moments without fully understanding the systems, struggles, and sacrifices happening around you. You don't know what your parents carry. You don't know what they fear. You don't know what they've already lost.

What you do know is what you see, what you feel, and what you absorb.

I learned early that life was not simple, even if it looked that way from the outside. There were unspoken lessons everywhere — in the tone of conversations, in the way adults reacted to stress, in what was said loudly and what was never said at all. Some lessons came gently. Others arrived hard and fast, without warning.

As a child, I was observant. I watched people closely. I paid attention to patterns, moods, and changes. I didn't always understand them, but I noticed them. I noticed how joy could exist one moment and disappear the next. I noticed how strength didn't always look like confidence, and how silence often meant more than words.

Growing up as an African American boy, I became aware — sometimes subtly, sometimes sharply — that the world saw me before it knew me. I didn't have the language for that awareness at first, but I felt it. There were expectations placed on me that I didn't choose. There were assumptions made before I opened my mouth. There were limits implied, even when they weren't spoken aloud.

At the same time, there was pride. There was history. There was resilience passed down whether I understood it or not. I came from people who endured, adapted, and survived. That strength didn't come with instructions — it came embedded in my DNA, waiting to be activated by experience.

As I moved through childhood, I learned how quickly innocence fades. Life introduces you to disappointment long before it explains why disappointment exists. You begin to realize that effort doesn't always equal reward, that doing the right thing doesn't guarantee the right outcome, and that fairness is not a universal rule.

There were moments of happiness, laughter, and belonging. Moments where the world felt wide open and full of possibility. And then there were moments where the world felt heavy, confusing, and unfair. Both were real. Both shaped me.

School became one of the first places where I learned about comparison. Who was faster. Who was smarter. Who was louder. Who was invisible. I learned where I fit — and where I didn't. I learned how quickly labels stick, and how difficult they are to remove once they've been placed on you.

I also learned about responsibility early. Whether through circumstance or expectation, I understood that life would not be handed to me. Whatever I wanted, I would have to reach for. Whatever I became, I would have to earn.

As I entered adolescence, the world grew louder. The stakes grew higher. Choices began to matter in ways they hadn't before. Every decision seemed to carry weight, even when I didn't fully understand the consequences. I was learning who I was, but I was also learning who I didn't want to be — and those two lessons don't always happen at the same pace.

There were times when I felt lost without knowing why. Times when I felt angry without understanding the source of that anger. Times when I questioned my place, my value, and my future. These weren't dramatic moments. They were quiet ones. Private ones. The kind you don't announce but carry silently.

Life has a way of introducing struggle gradually. It doesn't usually arrive all at once. It comes in pieces. Small disappointments. Broken expectations. Missed opportunities. And before you realize it, you're carrying more than you ever planned to.

Still, I kept moving forward. I learned to adapt. I learned to push through discomfort. I learned to survive emotionally before I learned how to heal. Like many people, I became good at functioning while hurting, at smiling while uncertain, at appearing strong even when I didn't feel it.

Looking back now, I see how every experience — good or bad — was shaping me for something I couldn't yet see. I see how life was teaching me lessons long before I understood their purpose. I see how resilience is often built quietly, without applause or recognition.

There were influences along the way — people who encouraged me, people who disappointed me, people who challenged me, and people who left marks on my life whether they intended to or not. Some lessons came through love. Others came through loss. Both were necessary.

As I grew older, I began to realize that life is not about avoiding pain — it's about learning what to do with it. It's about deciding whether pain will define you or refine you. That realization didn't come overnight. It came through years of living, failing, learning, and trying again.

November 16, 1978, was not just the day I was born. It was the beginning of a journey that would test my strength, my faith, my patience, and my understanding of what truly matters. It was the start of a life that would teach me — sometimes gently, sometimes brutally — the importance of life itself.

This book is not about perfection. It's about truth. It's about growth. It's about becoming. It's about the moments that nearly broke me and the moments that rebuilt me. It's about learning that life, no matter how difficult, still holds value — and that our stories matter, even when we don't think they do.

Chapter 1 is where my story begins — but it's also where understanding begins. Because before you can appreciate where you're going, you have to understand where you came from.

And this is where I came from.

CHAPTER 2
Lessons Learned the Hard Way

Life has a way of teaching its most important lessons without asking whether you're ready to learn them. Some lessons arrive gently, through guidance and care. Others arrive through pain, failure, and loss. For me, many of the lessons that shaped who I became were learned the hard way — through experience rather than instruction.

As I moved further into adulthood, the distance between who I thought I was and who I actually was began to widen. I carried confidence on the outside, but inside I was still searching for direction, purpose, and stability. I wanted success, peace, and meaning, but I didn't yet understand what those things truly required.

Mistakes became part of my education.

Some were small — poor decisions made in moments of impatience or pride. Others were larger, carrying consequences that lingered long after the moment had passed. What I didn't realize at the time was that every mistake was shaping my character, testing my resilience, and forcing me to confront parts of myself I would have preferred to ignore.

There were times when I trusted the wrong people. Times when I ignored warning signs because I wanted things to work out. Times when I chose comfort over growth, familiarity over progress. I learned that intentions don't protect you from consequences, and that good motives don't erase bad decisions.

I also learned how pride can quietly sabotage progress. Pride convinces you that you don't need help, that you can handle everything on your own, that asking for support is a weakness rather than a strength. For a long time, I carried that belief. I believed that self-reliance meant isolation, and that vulnerability was something to avoid.

That belief cost me.

It cost me relationships. It cost me opportunities. It cost me time I can never get back.

But it also taught me something valuable: strength is not about pretending you're unaffected. Strength is about honesty — with yourself first.

There were moments when life didn't go according to plan, moments when things fell apart despite my best efforts. Moments when I questioned whether I was moving forward or just standing still while time passed around me. Those moments were uncomfortable. They forced me to confront disappointment, regret, and frustration.

At times, I felt like I was running in place — busy but not productive, active but not fulfilled. I was doing things, but I wasn't always building something meaningful. That realization was hard to accept, because it challenged the story I told myself about who I was and where I was going.

Failure has a way of stripping away illusion.

I learned that success without purpose feels empty. I learned that ambition without direction leads to burnout. I learned that avoiding responsibility doesn't make it disappear — it just delays the reckoning.

There were relationships that ended not because there was no care, but because there was no alignment. There were conversations I avoided that should have happened sooner. There were apologies I needed to make, including some I needed to make to myself.

One of the hardest lessons was learning that you can't outrun yourself. No matter where you go, no matter what you achieve, the unresolved parts of you come along for the ride. Ignoring them doesn't make them disappear — it gives them more power.

I also learned that life doesn't pause while you figure things out. Bills still come. Responsibilities still exist. People still depend on you. The world keeps moving whether you feel prepared or not. That pressure can either break you or push you to grow.

For me, it did both — at different times.

There were moments when I felt overwhelmed, moments when the weight of expectation felt heavier than I knew how to carry. Moments when I questioned whether I was strong enough, smart enough, or capable enough to become the man I wanted to be.

But even in those moments, something inside me refused to quit.

Resilience doesn't always look heroic. Sometimes it looks like getting up when you don't feel motivated. Sometimes it looks like continuing forward even when confidence is low. Sometimes it looks like admitting you were wrong and choosing to do better.

I began to understand that lessons learned the hard way often stick the longest. They carve themselves into your memory because they come with emotional weight. They leave marks — not to punish you, but to remind you.

I learned to listen more carefully. To slow down. To question my assumptions. To examine my choices instead of blaming circumstances.

Accountability became less threatening and more empowering.

I also learned the value of humility. Humility doesn't mean thinking less of yourself — it means thinking of yourself honestly. It means recognizing your limitations without letting them define you. It means staying open to growth.

Some lessons arrived through loss. Loss of connection. Loss of trust. Loss of opportunities that might have turned out differently if I had been more aware, more patient, more prepared. Those losses hurt, but they also clarified what mattered.

They taught me that time is precious. That energy should be invested wisely. That not every path is meant to be taken, even if it looks appealing from a distance.

Through all of this, my understanding of life began to shift. I stopped seeing hardship as something to escape and started seeing it as something to learn from. I stopped measuring progress only by outcomes and started paying attention to growth.

I realized that life isn't about avoiding mistakes — it's about learning from them without letting them harden you. It's about allowing experience to deepen your wisdom rather than your bitterness.

The lessons I learned the hard way didn't make me perfect. They made me aware. They made me more intentional. They made me more compassionate — not just toward others, but toward myself.

Looking back, I wouldn't wish some of those moments on anyone. But I also wouldn't erase them. They shaped my understanding of responsibility, resilience, and the value of self-reflection.

They prepared me for the next phase of my life — the phase where I began to truly understand the importance of life, not as an abstract idea, but as a lived reality.

Because once you've fallen and stood back up, once you've faced your own shortcomings, once you've felt the cost of poor decisions, you begin to value life differently. You begin to move with more intention. You begin to choose growth over ego.

And that realization changed everything.

CHAPTER 3
The Importance of Life

There comes a point in life when you stop moving on autopilot. You may not recognize it immediately, but something changes. The noise quiets just enough for you to hear yourself think. The distractions lose their grip. And suddenly, you begin to understand that life is not guaranteed, time is not promised, and every moment carries weight.

For me, that realization didn't come all at once. It unfolded slowly, shaped by experience, loss, reflection, and moments of stillness that forced me to confront questions I had avoided for years. Questions about purpose. About direction. About why I was here at all.

I began to notice how fragile life really is. How quickly circumstances can change. How people you expect to always be there can suddenly be gone — physically, emotionally, or spiritually. I saw how plans collapse, how health can fail, how certainty can disappear without warning.

And with that awareness came a deeper understanding: life is not just something you pass through — it's something you are responsible for.

I started to reflect on the way I had been living. Not just what I was doing, but why I was doing it. Was I reacting to life, or was I choosing it? Was I living with intention, or simply surviving day to day?

There were moments when I realized how close I had come to wasting time — time spent worrying about things that didn't matter, holding onto resentment, chasing validation, or avoiding growth because it felt uncomfortable. I realized how easy it is to exist without truly living.

The importance of life became clearer when I understood that life doesn't need to be extraordinary to be meaningful. Meaning isn't found in constant achievement or recognition. It's found in awareness. In presence. In how you treat others. In how you treat yourself.

I began to see that every day I woke up was an opportunity — not a guarantee, not an entitlement, but an opportunity. An opportunity to choose better. To grow. To forgive. To learn. To contribute something positive, no matter how small.

There were moments when I thought about the version of myself I used to be — the one who believed time was unlimited, who assumed there would always be another chance, another day, another opportunity to make things right. That version of me didn't understand how precious life truly is.

Experience taught me otherwise.

I started paying closer attention to the people around me — their struggles, their resilience, their quiet strength. I noticed how everyone is carrying something, even when they don't show it. I learned that kindness matters more than being right, that listening matters more than speaking, and that presence matters more than perfection.

The importance of life also became clear in moments of pain. Pain has a way of stripping away illusion. It forces honesty. It demands attention. And while pain is never something we seek, it often becomes the teacher we didn't know we needed.

Through pain, I learned empathy. Through disappointment, I learned patience. Through loss, I learned gratitude. None of these lessons came easily, but all of them changed how I viewed life.

I began to understand that life is not about controlling outcomes — it's about controlling responses. You can't dictate everything that happens to you, but you can choose how you respond, how you grow, and how you move forward.

That realization was freeing.

It released me from the pressure of perfection. It allowed me to accept that mistakes are part of being human, that growth is a process, and that progress often looks messy before it looks successful.

I also began to reflect on legacy — not in terms of fame or accomplishment, but in terms of impact. How would I be remembered? What would people say about how I treated them? What would remain of me beyond titles, possessions, or achievements?

Those questions forced me to slow down and reevaluate my priorities. To align my actions with my values. To live in a way that reflected what I claimed to believe.

Life started to feel less like a race and more like a responsibility.

I became more intentional with my time. More selective with my energy. More aware of the choices I made daily. I learned that saying no is sometimes necessary, that rest is not weakness, and that growth requires honesty.

The importance of life also meant accepting its uncertainty. Accepting that there are no guarantees, no perfect paths, no absolute security. But instead of fear, that uncertainty began to inspire gratitude.

Because if nothing is guaranteed, then everything matters.

Every conversation. Every decision. Every moment of connection. Every chance to learn. Every opportunity to show compassion.

I began to live with a deeper sense of presence. To appreciate moments that once felt ordinary. To value people not for what they could do for me, but for who they were. To recognize that life's meaning often reveals itself in quiet moments, not dramatic ones.

There were still challenges. Still setbacks. Still moments of doubt. But my perspective had changed. I no longer saw difficulty as evidence of failure — I saw it as part of the process of becoming.

The importance of life isn't something you're taught once and remember forever. It's something you relearn repeatedly, through experience, reflection, and growth. It evolves as you do.

And as I embraced that truth, I felt more grounded. More intentional. More alive.

Life was no longer something happening to me. It was something I was actively participating in.

That shift marked a turning point — a movement away from survival and toward purpose. Toward growth. Toward meaning.

THE BOOK OF STEVE

And it set the foundation for the next chapter of my life — one rooted in reflection, faith, and self-discovery.

CHAPTER 4
Growth, Faith, and Self-Discovery

Growth rarely announces itself when it begins. It doesn't arrive with certainty or clarity. Most of the time, growth starts quietly — in moments of discomfort, reflection, and unanswered questions. For me, growth became unavoidable once I stopped running from myself and started paying attention to what life was trying to teach me.

There came a point when I realized that change wasn't optional. Staying the same was no longer safe, comfortable, or honest. I could feel the tension between who I had been and who I was becoming. That tension wasn't pleasant, but it was necessary.

Growth demanded that I slow down and look inward.

For a long time, I focused on external things — what I was achieving, how I was perceived, whether I was meeting expectations. But eventually, I understood that external progress means very little without internal alignment. You can move forward in life and still be lost if you don't know who you are.

Self-discovery required honesty. It required me to acknowledge my fears, my flaws, and my patterns. It required me to confront habits that no longer served me and beliefs that limited my growth. Some of those realizations were uncomfortable. Some were humbling. All were necessary.

Faith began to play a deeper role during this time — not as a rigid set of rules, but as a source of grounding and perspective. Faith became less about answers and more about trust. Trust in the process. Trust that growth often happens before understanding. Trust that purpose unfolds over time.

I learned that faith doesn't eliminate doubt — it coexists with it. Doubt doesn't mean a lack of belief; it often means a desire for truth. And in that space between certainty and uncertainty, I found room to grow.

Reflection became a regular part of my life. I began asking myself hard questions:
Was I living in alignment with my values?
Was I reacting to life, or responding thoughtfully?
Was I open to growth, or clinging to comfort?

These questions didn't always have immediate answers, but they guided my decisions. They helped me become more intentional with my choices and more aware of my motivations.

I also learned the importance of solitude. Not isolation, but intentional time alone — time to think, to process, to listen. In those quiet moments, I began to hear my own voice more clearly. Not the voice shaped by expectation or pressure, but the voice rooted in authenticity.

Growth required patience. I had to accept that transformation doesn't happen overnight. It happens gradually, through consistency and commitment. Through small decisions repeated daily. Through choosing growth even when it feels slow or unseen.

Faith supported that patience. It reminded me that progress isn't always visible, and that planting seeds doesn't produce immediate results. Sometimes growth happens beneath the surface long before it shows outwardly.

There were moments when I felt uncertain about the path ahead. Moments when I questioned whether I was making the right choices. But those moments no longer paralyzed me. Instead, they encouraged reflection and recalibration.

I began to understand that self-discovery is not about reinventing yourself — it's about uncovering who you already are beneath layers of expectation, fear, and conditioning. It's about returning to what matters most.

Growth also meant learning to forgive — both others and myself. Forgiveness wasn't about excusing behavior or forgetting the past. It was about releasing the emotional weight that held me back. It was about choosing peace over resentment.

Faith helped me understand forgiveness as an act of strength rather than weakness. It allowed me to let go of bitterness and focus on forward movement.

As I continued to grow, I became more comfortable with uncertainty. I accepted that life doesn't offer guarantees, only opportunities. And I learned to meet those opportunities with intention rather than fear.

Self-discovery also deepened my empathy. As I became more aware of my own struggles, I became more understanding of others'. I recognized that everyone is navigating something unseen. That realization changed how I interacted with people — more patience, more compassion, more grace.

Growth reshaped my definition of success. Success became less about external validation and more about internal peace. Less about comparison and more about alignment. Less about achievement and more about integrity.

Faith, growth, and self-discovery became interconnected. Each supported the other. Faith grounded me. Growth challenged me. Self-discovery clarified me.

Together, they helped me become more intentional about the life I was building.

I began to live with greater awareness — not just of my actions, but of my thoughts, my reactions, and my intentions. I learned that awareness is the foundation of growth. You can't change what you don't acknowledge.

This phase of my life wasn't dramatic or flashy. It was quiet, steady, and deeply transformative. It was about becoming more honest, more grounded, and more present.

And through that process, I began to truly understand who I was becoming — not the version shaped by circumstance, but the version shaped by choice.

That understanding set the stage for the next chapter — the chapter where identity, resilience, and purpose came together.

CHAPTER 5
Becoming Steven Robertson

Becoming yourself is not a single moment. It is a process — one shaped by experience, reflection, and choice. For a long time, I thought becoming meant reaching a destination, achieving a certain status, or finally feeling complete. What I eventually learned is that becoming is ongoing. It's not about arrival; it's about alignment.

As I reflected on my life, I began to see the common thread running through every season: resilience. Not the loud, dramatic kind, but the quiet kind that shows up when you keep going despite uncertainty, disappointment, or fatigue. The kind that doesn't seek recognition but refuses to quit.

Resilience shaped me long before I recognized it. It showed up in how I adapted, how I learned, and how I kept moving forward even when progress felt slow. It showed up in my willingness to confront myself and grow.

Becoming Steven Robertson meant accepting my past without being defined by it. It meant acknowledging my mistakes without letting them dictate my future. It meant understanding that growth doesn't erase where you've been — it gives it meaning.

I began to take ownership of my story. Not just the parts I was proud of, but the parts that challenged me. Ownership brought clarity. It allowed me to move forward without carrying shame or regret.

Identity became less about labels and more about values. I stopped asking who I was supposed to be and started asking who I wanted to be. That shift changed everything.

I wanted to be someone who lived with intention. Someone who valued integrity over convenience. Someone who understood the importance of life — not just in theory, but in action.

Purpose became clearer as I aligned my actions with my values. Purpose wasn't something I had to search for — it was something I had to live. It showed up in how I treated others, how I made decisions, and how I used my time.

I learned that purpose doesn't always come with certainty. Sometimes it comes with commitment — to growth, to honesty, to contribution. Purpose is less about knowing the outcome and more about choosing the direction.

Becoming myself also meant letting go of comparison. Comparison distracts you from your own path and steals your appreciation for progress. Once I stopped measuring myself against others, I became more focused, more grounded, and more content.

I accepted that my journey wouldn't look like anyone else's. That acceptance brought peace.

Resilience continued to be tested. Life didn't suddenly become easier because my perspective changed. Challenges still appeared. Setbacks still happened. But my response was different. I faced difficulty with awareness rather than avoidance.

I learned that strength doesn't mean you never struggle — it means you don't let struggle define you. It means you keep choosing growth even when it's uncomfortable.

Becoming Steven Robertson meant embracing responsibility — not as a burden, but as empowerment. Responsibility gave me agency. It reminded me that while I can't control everything, I can control my choices.

I also became more comfortable with vulnerability. Sharing my story — honestly and without embellishment — became an act of strength. Vulnerability creates connection. It reminds us that we are not alone in our struggles or our growth.

As my identity became clearer, so did my sense of direction. I wasn't chasing validation anymore. I was building alignment. I wasn't trying to prove myself — I was becoming myself.

This chapter of my life was marked by intention. By conscious decisions. By reflection. By commitment to living in a way that reflected what mattered most.

I began to see my life not as a series of random events, but as a narrative — one shaped by choice, resilience, and growth. Every experience, even the difficult ones, contributed to who I was becoming.

Becoming Steven Robertson didn't mean I had everything figured out. It meant I was willing to keep learning. To keep growing. To stay honest with myself.

And that willingness mattered more than certainty.

This phase of becoming prepared me for the final chapter — not an ending, but a continuation. A forward-looking perspective rooted in hope, intention, and responsibility.

CHAPTER 6
Looking Forward: The Life I Choose

Looking forward does not mean forgetting where you've been. It means carrying what you've learned without being weighed down by it. As I think about the life ahead of me, I do so with awareness — aware of the past, grounded in the present, and intentional about the future.

I no longer believe that life is something that simply happens. Life is shaped by choice. Every day offers decisions that either move you closer to who you want to be or keep you tied to who you used to be. Understanding that truth changed how I approach each moment.

The life I choose is rooted in intention.

I choose to live with awareness — aware of my thoughts, my actions, and my impact. Awareness keeps me present. It reminds me that how I show up matters, even in small moments. Especially in small moments.

I choose growth over comfort. Comfort can be tempting, but growth is necessary. Growth challenges me to stretch beyond what feels easy, to remain open to learning, and to continue evolving as a person. I understand now that growth doesn't end — it adapts.

I choose responsibility — not as a burden, but as empowerment. Responsibility gives me agency over my life. It reminds me that while I can't control every circumstance, I can control my response. That understanding gives me strength.

The life I choose values connection. I choose to invest in relationships that are honest, supportive, and aligned with mutual respect. I understand that meaningful connection requires effort, communication, and vulnerability. And I am willing to show up fully.

I also choose peace. Peace doesn't mean the absence of conflict or challenge — it means choosing clarity over chaos, understanding over reaction, and purpose over distraction. Peace is something I protect through boundaries and intention.

The future is uncertain, but uncertainty no longer frightens me. I've learned that uncertainty is part of life's design. It keeps us humble. It keeps us adaptable. It keeps us present.

I choose to approach uncertainty with curiosity rather than fear.

The life I choose also honors the importance of life itself. I don't take time for granted. I understand that each day is an opportunity — one that deserves respect and attention. I aim to live in a way that reflects gratitude, even during difficult seasons.

I choose reflection. Reflection keeps me aligned. It allows me to evaluate my choices, learn from experience, and adjust when necessary. Reflection ensures that I remain honest with myself.

I choose integrity. Integrity means living in alignment with my values, even when no one is watching. It means choosing honesty over convenience and principle over approval.

I choose compassion — toward others and toward myself. Compassion acknowledges that we are all learning, growing, and navigating life in our own way. It allows space for grace.

Looking forward, I don't expect perfection. I expect progress. I expect learning. I expect growth. And I accept that setbacks will happen. What matters is how I respond to them.

The life I choose is not defined by titles, achievements, or recognition. It is defined by intention, awareness, and contribution. By how I treat others. By how I treat myself.

If this book offers anything to the reader, I hope it offers this understanding: your life matters. Your story matters. And you have the power to choose how you live.

Becoming Steven Robertson is not a completed task — it's an ongoing commitment. A commitment to growth. To honesty. To purpose.

As I move forward, I do so with gratitude — for the lessons, the challenges, the growth, and the opportunity to keep choosing.

This is the life I choose. I hold tight to the love I chose. I keep walking with God, who first chose me. And, I keep putting my best effort in everything I do because I know that is what a real man should always do.

CHAPTER 7
Choosing Health, Choosing Love

There comes a point in life when survival is no longer the goal — sustainability is. When you realize that getting through the day is not enough if the way you are living is slowly taking something from you. For me, that realization came through my health — both physical and mental — and through the love and partnership I share with my wife.

Hypertension is not loud. It doesn't always announce itself with dramatic symptoms. It lives quietly in the body, applying pressure where pressure does not belong. For a long time, I treated it like a background issue — something to manage later, something to think about tomorrow. But tomorrow kept coming, and the responsibility kept growing.

At the same time, mental health challenges were demanding attention in ways I could no longer ignore. Stress, anxiety, emotional fatigue — these things don't disappear just because you're strong or determined. They require intention. They require care. They require honesty.

I had to accept that my body and my mind were asking me to slow down, to listen, and to take responsibility for the life I was living.

That acceptance was not easy.

There is a pride many men carry — the belief that we should be able to push through anything, that rest is weakness, that asking for help means failure. I carried that belief for a long time. And it cost me more than I realized.

My wife and I reached a point where we had to have honest conversations — not just about health, but about how we wanted to live. We didn't want to wait for a crisis to force change. We wanted to choose it.

So we committed together.

We committed to being more intentional about what we put into our bodies. That meant eating out less — not because eating out is wrong, but because it had become too easy, too frequent, and too unhealthy. We committed to cutting back on junk food, not as punishment, but as respect for our bodies.

We made the decision to stop treating sweets like daily necessities. They became occasional choices instead of habits. We started paying closer attention to how much pasta and bread we were eating — not eliminating them, but learning moderation.

And one of the simplest but most meaningful changes: we stopped drinking soda pop every day. It sounds small, but small changes add up. They say to your body, I care about you. They say to your future, I want you to be better than my past.

These choices weren't about restriction. They were about intention.

Mental health required just as much attention. I had to learn to recognize when I was overwhelmed, when I was emotionally exhausted, and when I needed to pause instead of push. I had to accept that rest is not laziness and that boundaries are not rejection.

My wife and I also committed to taking more time for each other — and for ourselves. Life has a way of pulling couples into survival mode, where everything becomes about responsibilities, schedules, and obligations. We wanted to move back toward connection.

That meant carving out time to talk. Time to laugh. Time to simply be together without distraction. It also meant giving each other permission to take time alone when needed — without guilt.

Another hard but necessary commitment was learning to say no.

There are people we love deeply — children we want to see, moments we don't want to miss, opportunities we wish we could say yes to. But there are times when the body simply does not have the strength. And pretending otherwise only leads to harm.

We learned to let people know when we weren't able to do something — whether that meant babysitting, attending events, or taking on responsibilities we physically couldn't manage. Saying no didn't mean we didn't care. It meant we were being honest.

Honesty protects health. Honesty preserves dignity.

One of the most humbling parts of my journey has been learning to rely on others for transportation. Not having a vehicle challenged my independence in ways I wasn't prepared for. It forced me to confront pride head-on.

At first, it was uncomfortable. I worried about being a burden. I worried about how people saw me. I worried about asking too much.

But over time, something changed.

I began to see the generosity in people's willingness to help. I saw the sincerity in their offers. I felt the care behind their actions. And I learned to receive help with gratitude instead of shame.

People took time out of their lives to take us to run errands, to visit us, to take us places — not because they had to, but because they wanted to. That realization softened something in me.

I learned that receiving help is not weakness — it is connection.

I committed myself to being more reflective, especially when frustration or disappointment surfaced. Instead of being quick to blame others or circumstances, I began to look inward first. I asked myself: What is my responsibility here? What can I control? What can I learn?

That shift changed how I saw myself — and how others saw me.

I can see the respect people have for me. I can hear the sincerity when they ask if they can help. I can feel the love when they tell me they care about me.

And I believe — truly believe — that they can feel my love too. They can feel my good heart. Love is not just spoken. It is felt in presence, in gratitude, in humility.

This chapter of my life has taught me that being a man is not about carrying everything alone. It's about knowing when to stand and when to lean. It's about protecting your health so you can show up fully for the people who matter.

My hope is that this book — and especially this chapter — helps other men face the vulnerable and limited parts of themselves. Not with shame, but with honesty. Because vulnerability is where connection lives. And connection is where healing begins.

When men allow themselves to be supported, they become stronger partners, stronger friends, stronger family members. They become more present. More grounded. More loving.

That is what I strive for — to be the best man possible for the people close to me. Not the toughest. Not the most self-sufficient. But the most intentional, the most loving, the most honest.

Choosing health is choosing life.
Choosing love is choosing connection.
And choosing vulnerability is choosing growth.

This is the commitment I live with now — and the legacy I hope to leave behind. I share these life lessons with the young men I mentor, and with any males my age who are willing to listen. A lot of men say they want to be able to move in strength and peace the way they see I do. I tell them they can, and you can too.

I'll end this book by giving you some tips to help you be the BEST version of the man you are too. You have had to overcome a lot and you will always have things to overcome. My life is far from perfect but I have been able to find my perfect peace despite that. It's mainly because when you KNOW FOR A FACT you are doing your very best, you can get out of the way quicker to let God do the rest.

50 Ways To Be A BEST Man

1. **Be honest**, even when the truth is uncomfortable.

2. **Listen without fixing** — sometimes presence matters more than solutions.

3. **Take responsibility** for your actions, choices, and reactions.

4. **Protect your health** so you can be present for those who need you.

5. **Show affection openly** — love is not weakness.

6. **Respect boundaries**, including your own.

7. **Admit when you're wrong** and apologize without excuses.

8. **Stay teachable** — growth doesn't end with age.

9. **Value consistency** over empty promises.

10. **Express gratitude** to those who support you.

11. **Provide emotional safety**, not just physical presence.

12. **Choose patience** when frustration rises.
13. **Care for your mental health** as seriously as your physical health.
14. **Model self-respect** so others learn how to treat you.
15. **Be dependable**, even in small things.
16. **Encourage others**, especially when they doubt themselves.
17. **Allow yourself to be helped** without shame.
18. **Lead with example**, not control.
19. **Honor your commitments**, or communicate when you can't.
20. **Speak kindly**, especially in conflict.
21. **Make time for the people you love**, not just the work you do.
22. **Protect your peace** by choosing what deserves your energy.
23. **Forgive without keeping score**.
24. **Stay grounded in humility**, not ego.

25. **Show up emotionally**, not just physically.
26. **Be gentle with yourself** — strength includes compassion.
27. **Respect women** through actions, not words alone.
28. **Model accountability** for younger men watching you.
29. **Choose growth over comfort**.
30. **Be slow to blame** and quick to reflect.
31. **Care how your words land**, not just how they're spoken.
32. **Stand firm in values**, even when it costs you.
33. **Create space for vulnerability** in yourself and others.
34. **Love without conditions**, manipulation, or control.
35. **Practice self-discipline**, not punishment.
36. **Be emotionally present** during difficult conversations.
37. **Accept limitations** without losing self-worth.

38. **Honor partnership** by sharing effort, not keeping score.
39. **Respect differences** without needing dominance.
40. **Be reliable in crisis**, calm when others are overwhelmed.
41. **Speak life into others**, especially family.
42. **Protect your integrity** when no one is watching.
43. **Choose kindness** even when you could choose power.
44. **Lead with love**, not fear.
45. **Rest when your body and mind ask for it**.
46. **Value connection** more than control.
47. **Accept love freely**, without suspicion or pride.
48. **Encourage independence** while offering support.
49. **Leave people better** than you found them.
50. **Live in a way that says: "You are safe, seen, and valued with me."**

THE BOOK OF STEVE

THE ART & ARTISTS

THE BOOK

Life is not defined by limitations. It is defined by how we choose to live. In his second powerful book, **THE BOOK OF STEVE**, Steve Robertson of Mississippi continues his journey with honesty, depth, and purpose. Released in January 2026, this deeply personal work explores the realities of living, growing, and finding meaning  through adversity while honoring the value of every life, regardless of circumstance.

This book is not about perfection. It is about resilience. It is about choice. It is about the importance of life — even when life is difficult.

Written with clarity and compassion, Steve Robertson shares lived experience shaped by hardship, reflection, and growth. His voice speaks directly to readers who have felt overlooked, underestimated, or defined by challenges beyond their control — especially within the disabled community, where strength is often quiet and perseverance is daily.

With assistance from BePublished.org, a publishing firm created in 2003 that's dedicated to supporting underrepresented and disabled voices, **THE BOOK OF STEVE** this book stands as both a personal testimony and a message of inclusion, dignity, and hope.

Inside these pages, readers will find:

- A real-life perspective on overcoming adversity without denial or exaggeration
- Honest reflections on purpose, responsibility, and self-worth
- Encouragement for individuals living with disabilities and chronic challenges

- A reminder that life has value at every stage and in every condition

This book is for:

- Readers seeking inspiration rooted in truth
- Members of the disabled community looking to feel seen and respected
- Anyone navigating hardship, uncertainty, or personal growth
- Those who believe that every life deserves meaning and voice

Steve Robertson does not offer easy answers. He offers something more powerful—understanding, presence, and the courage to keep choosing life. Order your copy of **THE BOOK OF STEVE** today.

This book is written in solidarity with the disabled community, chronic illness warriors, caregivers, and loved ones who walk beside them. Your life matters. Your pace matters. Your story matters.

Available as an ebook for $5.95, **THE BOOK OF STEVE** by Steve Robertson may also be purchased worldwide as a paperback for $14.95 from bricks-and-mortar and online book retailers including Barnes & Noble, your local bookstore, Amazon.com, and BePublished.org.

THE AUTHOR

Steve Robertson, a Mississippi native and lifelong Brookhaven resident, is a "Jack of all trades, and master of each" who graduated with a 3.0 GPA from Brookhaven High School. A professional laborer who is able to assist with completing everything from landscaping tasks to renovating homes and government buildings, Steve is also a master cook who enjoys grilling and entertaining family and friends.

Taking up a challenge issued by his sister-in-law in February 2025, Steve wrote and released his first book (<u>THE IMPORTANCE OF YOUR LIFE</u>) so share a message on his heart. The father of two penned his entire book is less than an hour! On January 6, 2026, he and his wife completed a Book Bang workshop through The Writers Consortium's partnership with BePublished.org – where she created their book covers and they each wrote their new books. His second book, <u>**THE BOOK OF STEVE**</u>, was released that same month.

Steve's favorite color is blue but his favorite gift is his grandson. Steven is also a great vocalist, although he usually tries to hide this talent from others due to his general shyness.

"He is the sweetest man alive," his wife, Author Latisha A. Jefferson-Robertson, maintains. "I thank God for blessing me with this man's love every single day."

THE PROOFREADER/COVER DESIGNER

Latisha A. Jefferson-Robertson, a Mississippi native, is an accomplished entrepreneur and celebrated vocalist who performed at Carnegie Hall while a teen member of an award-winning choir at a school in Jackson, Mississippi.

The former Atlanta resident is the author of **The Artistic Sketch Of Me** (a mini-collection of selected poetry published in 2009). A decade later, in 2019, she released her second book titled **This Kindred Heart of Mine** – which also included prose. The following year, in 2020, Latisha wrote **What A Day! What A Day!** one evening in February when challenged to complete a book in 24 hours. The professional proofreader for BePublished.org rose to the challenge!

Latisha wrote her fourth book the same way, alongside her husband, author Steve Robertson, in February 2025 – releasing **Kids Gone Wild** the same week her husband's debut **The Importance Of Your Life** was released worldwide by BePublished.org in March 2025.

On January 6, 2026, she and her husband completed a Book Bang workshop through The Writers Consortium's partnership with BePublished.org -- where she created their book covers and they each wrote their new books. As a result, her fifth book, **MY EVEERYDAY LIFE**, was released that same month.

When she's not busy volunteering to assist the sick/elderly or tending children, Latisha enjoys spending her free time listening to music, playing Spades and chess, watching movies, enjoying good food, and spending time with loved ones.

A relative of professional football greats including the legendary Walter "Sweetness" Payton and Lynn Swan, Latisha Jefferson-Robertson is currently working on other projects where her creativity lends itself to jewelry making, writing songs, and learning to use AI to perform songs that teach valuable lessons to children.

www.ingramcontent.com/pod-product-compliance
Lightning Source LLC
LaVergne TN
LVHW051209080426
835512LV00019B/3182